Calligraphy

ABCde
KLMN
STUV

fFGbIJ

opqr

wxyz

Creative Crafts

Calligraphy

John Lancaster

Consultant: Henry Pluckrose

Photography: Chris Fairclough

FRANKLIN WATTS
LONDON • SYDNEY

This edition 2004

Franklin Watts
96 Leonard Street
London EC2A 4XD

Franklin Watts Australia
45-51 Huntley Street
Alexandria, NSW 2015

Hardback edition published
in the Fresh Start series
as Decorated Lettering.

Design: K and Co
Editor: Jenny Wood

Acknowledgement
I owe thanks to Henry Pluckrose
for his advice and help as well as
to Chris Fairclough for his
splendid photographic work.
Otherwise, I must pay my deepest
respect to the countless medieval
scribes who have endowed the
world with beautiful art treasures
– often written and decorated in
cold and ill-lit scriptoria in
monastic houses and abbeys
throughout Europe many
centuries ago. Their work has
been an inspiration to modern
calligraphers and I hope that all of
you will be stimulated by their
endeavours and go on to produce
some lovely work yourself.
John Lancaster

The author and publishers would
like to thank the following for their
kind permission to reproduce
copyright material: The Bodleian
Library, page 7 (top right); The
Dean and Chapter of Durham
Cathedral, page 28.

ISBN: 0 7496 5894 0

Printed in Belgium

Contents

Equipment and materials 4
Getting ready 5
The writing position 7
Using a guidesheet 9
Practising written forms 11
Writing different medieval scripts 12
Roman Square Capitals 12
Rustic Lettering 14
Uncial and Half-Uncial scripts 16
Round Hand 19
Gothic Black Letters 23
Writing on parchment 25
Designing a decorated letter 28
Designing a decorated border 32
On your own 34
Further information 38
A brief history of calligraphy 39
Index 40

Equipment and materials

Brush (watercolour type, No 5)
Card
Craft knife
Elastic bands
Fibre-tipped pens (a range of
    colours)
Inks (see page 5 for further
    details)
Masking tape
Paper – white typing paper, A4
        – hand-made (hot-pressed)
            paper for special work
Paper clips
Parchment (off-cuts of
parchment and vellum, see page
38 for suppliers)
Pens (see page 5 for further
details)
Pencil (HB or H)

Pounce (for treating parchment
and vellum, see pages 25-27 for
further details)
Quills (These are not essential
but it is useful to try cutting a
quill and writing with it. Look on
the web for instructions, e.g.
www.osv.org/kids/crafts5.htm,
and ask an adult for help.)
Ruler (wooden, plastic or metal)
Scissors
Tracing paper
Work table
Writing board (either a sheet of
hardboard or plywood, or a
strong sheet of card, size
approximately 38cm x 28cm, 15″
x 11″)

'Calligraphy' really means the skillful production of beautiful letters. The art goes back to medieval times and many wonderful examples can still be seen today. Calligraphy is a fascinating, inexpensive and satisfying activity for all ages. I hope you enjoy it.

Pens

The lettering styles shown in this book are formed using an 'edged' pen. This type of pen usually has a square end (edge) or writing point, but some have an oblique edge for producing styles known as 'Rustic' and 'Uncial'. When you write with an edged pen, it produces the thick and thin strokes which give the lettering its special and quite distinctive character.

You can buy italic pens at artists' materials shops or at the places listed on page 38. Here are some suggested edged pens. Use pen sizes 2.0, 3.5 and 5mm.
1. Berol fibre-tipped Italic Pens
2. Edding 1255 Calligraphy Pens
3. Zig Kuretake Calligraphy Pens
4. Manuscript

You will also be asked to use a dip pen, so-called because it has to be dipped into ink. A dip pen consists of a penholder (plastic or wood), a metal nib and a brass reservoir which is attached underneath the nib to hold small quantities of ink. Here are some suggested dip pens:
1. Coit
2. Brause
3. Speedball
4. Chronicle
5. William & Mitchell Round Hand Pens

Inks

You will need black and coloured fountain pen inks, as well as Daler-Rowney's jet black India Calli ink. This ink, along with other calligraphy inks, has been formulated to flow easily and smoothly in the pen. Calligraphy inks should be used with dip pens.

Paper

The lettering craftsmen or 'scribes' who wrote manuscript books, legal documents, letters and other texts in the great monasteries in medieval times, wrote with quill pens and black and coloured inks on parchment or vellum.

You will be told where to obtain small samples of

parchment or vellum and how to prepare these for writing on. This will give you an opportunity to experience what it is like to write on these materials. They are expensive, however, so most of your writing will be done on paper.

Writing styles

Writing styles have developed and changed throughout history. Our alphabet originated in the Middle East, in Persia (now Iran). It then came westwards through Egypt, Greece and Italy.

This book introduces you to five medieval scripts. I hope that learning to write these will lead you to enjoy looking at examples of medieval manuscript books. And when you are familiar with the different scripts, you may find that you can begin to place these manuscript books in their correct historical period.

Decorated letters

The manuscripts written in the Middle Ages were very beautifully decorated. The scribes used gold leaf and bright egg-tempera colours in designing the illustrations and decorations

which 'illuminate' the pages, and they made a great deal of use of decorated letters.

Try designing some decorated borders and letters of your own. You will find some instructions and ideas on pages 28-37.

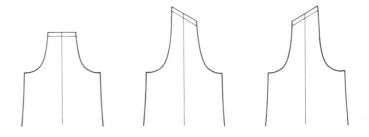

1 The pen on the left has a square edge, while the two on the right have oblique edges.

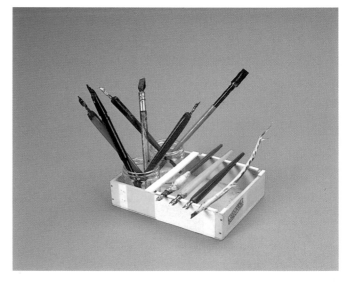

2 A simple, home-made pen rack is very helpful for keeping all your pens together.

It is most important to be comfortable when you write. You should sit on a chair (one without arms) or on a stool. Rest your writing board in your lap, with the board placed against your worktable at an angle of about 40-45°. Writing on a sloping surface means that you will not get tired quickly. It also allows you to control your pen much more easily.

1 (Top right) In the medieval scriptoria (the name given to the studio-workshops in which the scribes worked), each scribe sat at a sloping desk. He wrote with a quill pen in his right hand and held his parchment sheets flat on the sloping surface with a bone point or uncut feather in his left hand.

2 (Right) Tape a sheet of paper or thin card across your writing board so that you can use its top edge as a 'writing guide'. The sheet of paper on which you intend to write can slide underneath.

3 You can make a similar writing board using two pieces of card and two elastic bands. Place the smaller sheet on top of the larger sheet and use the elastic bands to hold it in place.

4 Slide your writing paper under the smaller piece of card.

5 Hold the pen in your writing hand. If you use your right hand the shaft of the pen will point over your right shoulder.

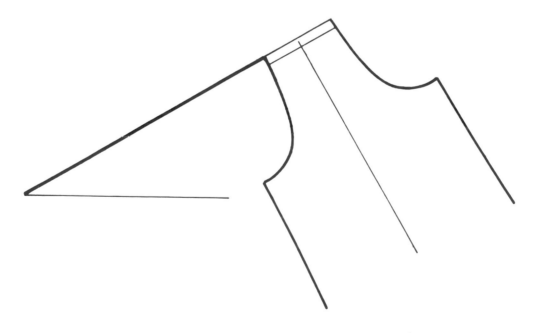

6 You will find that the square writing edge of the pen sits at an angle of 30° to the horizontal writing line. This is probably the best position. (The position of the pen changes for Rustic and Uncial scripts – see pages 14-18.)

If you write with your left hand, you will either need to twist the paper to suit your style of writing or use a left-handed oblique pen.

Guidelines will ensure that your lines of lettering are well spaced and straight. Medieval scribes used to draw such lines on their pages of parchment or vellum using a bone point and a ruler. Occasionally they used coloured inks.

A special guidesheet has been prepared to assist you (see page 10). It has been designed for use with a 5.00mm fibre-tipped pen.

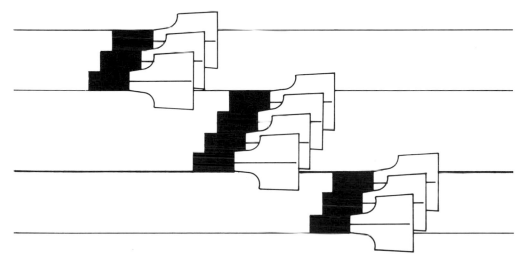

1 The size of a letter is determined by the width of your pen's square writing edge. Capital letters, for instance, are seven pen widths high from the writing lines. The body of a lower-case letter is four pen widths.

2 Place an A4 sheet of white paper over the guidesheet, attaching it with two paper clips. The guidelines should show through and give you a basis for your writing. (Or make your own guidesheet by copying the one on page 10 on to a sheet of strong white paper.)

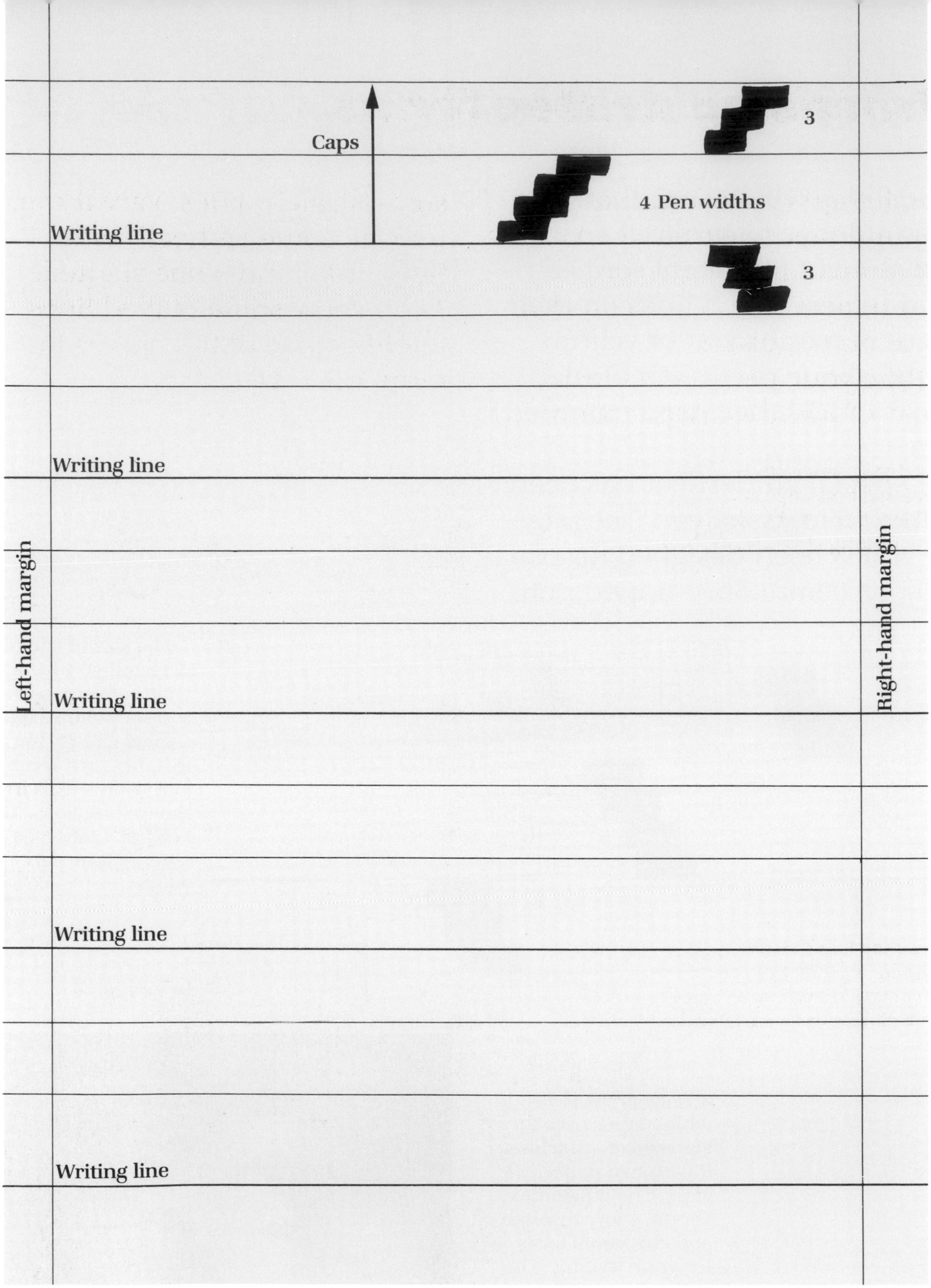

Caps

4 Pen widths

3

3

Writing line

Writing line

Left-hand margin

Right-hand margin

Writing line

Writing line

Writing line

A helpful tip

If you don't want to use a guidesheet, you should rule each page of writing paper in a similar way.

A calligrapher always spends a few minutes practising pen patterns and letters before commencing work. You should try to do the same.

Take your pen and a clean sheet of white A4 paper. Draw some straight lines. Vary these, making some vertical, some horizontal and some slanted. Then draw some curved lines, joining some of the curves to form letter 'O's.

1 Practising pen patterns and letters will build up your confidence and help you get into a 'writing rhythm'.

2 You may like to write a complete alphabet as one of your practice exercises. If not, then write at least ten letters.

Writing different medieval scripts

When you first attempt to write the five medieval 'writing hands' or 'scripts', start with a 5.00mm fibre-tipped pen. Fibre-tipped pens are easier to handle than dip pens, but as you progress you may wish to go on to dip pens and quills. Eventually you should try a range of pens, to find out which you prefer.

The five medieval scripts you will be learning to write are:
1 SQUARE CAPITALS (Roman)
2 RUSTIC LETTERS (Roman)
3 UNCIAL and HALF-UNCIAL SCRIPTS (Irish and English)
4 ROUND HAND (Continental and English)
5 GOTHIC BLACK LETTERS (European and English)

These are different writing styles. They were created as writing developed through the centuries. They range from the 'Roman Square Capitals' of the first century AD (often referred to simply as 'Roman Caps'), right through to the fifteenth-century 'Gothic Black'.

Roman Square Capitals

The scribes who lived and worked in Roman times wrote with square-edged reeds or quills. The pen-made letters which they produced were known as *Capitalis Quadrata*, now translated as 'Square Capitals' or 'Square Caps'. These letters were written slowly. They are similar to the beautiful Roman Capitals used on inscriptions carved into the stone and marble of triumphal arches, tombstones, altars, buildings and monuments.

How to write Square Capitals
Prepare your writing board with an A4 sheet of white paper clipped over your guidesheet. You will also need your 5.00mm fibre-tipped pen. (The guidesheet on page 10 was designed for a 5.00mm fibre-tipped pen, so if you decide to use another size or type of pen, you will need to draw out a new guidesheet.)

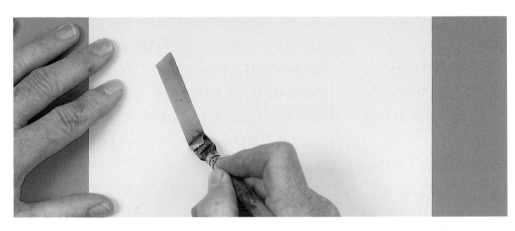

1 Hold the pen at the normal writing angle of 30° to the writing line. This angle should never vary. It is essential to be absolutely consistent.

2 Here you can see how a square-edged pen produces both thick and thin strokes when held at the normal writing angle.

3 Copy the examples shown here but keep the letters strong and round. The numbers tell you the order in which you should do the strokes. The arrows show you in which direction to move the pen. The alphabet of Roman Square Caps shown here was written freely with a dip pen, but you should use your fibre-tipped pen to start with.

ABCDEFGHIJK
LMNOPQRST
VWXYZ

Rustic Lettering

Another type of pen lettering is known as Rustic Lettering. Roman scribes wrote it until the fifth century AD. It was a style used in manuscript books as well as for everyday writing.

Rustic Letters and Square Caps have some similarities. They are both simple capital letter forms. But they differ because in writing Rustic Letters the scribes either used pens with an oblique or slanted edge or turned their square-edged pens to form thinnish verticals and thickish horizontal strokes. This means that Rustic Letters are quite different in character from Square Caps.

How to write Rustic Letters
Prepare your writing board with an A4 sheet of white paper clipped over your guidesheet. You will also need an edged pen.

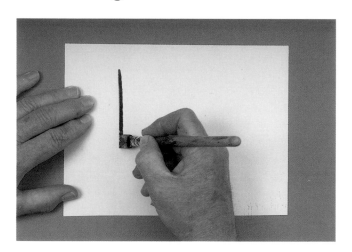

1 Holding an oblique-edged pen in the normal way will produce thin verticals and thick horizontals. Here, a square-edged poster pen has been turned sideways so that thin verticals and…

2 …thick horizontals result.

3 As you write Rustic Letters, compress them slightly. They are not quite as round and formal as Square Caps.

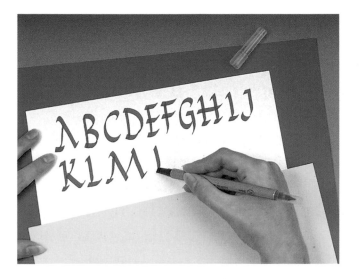

ABCDEFGHIJ
KLMNOPQR
STVWXYZ

4 Copy the examples shown here. The numbers tell you the order in which you should do the strokes. The arrows show you in which direction to move the pen.

Uncial and Half-Uncial scripts

These open, round pen letters were used mainly by monks in Ireland and Northern England. They were quicker to write than Square Caps or Rustic Letters. Remember to try to make them round in shape.

The first Uncial Letters were exactly one Roman inch (an *uncia*) in height. This is how they got their name. Half-Uncial Letters were the first to have *ascending* and *descending* strokes (the top and bottom parts of letters such as b, h and y, for example). Our lower-case letters developed from them.

How to write Uncial and Half-Uncial Letters

As before, prepare your writing board with a fresh sheet of white A4 paper clipped over your guidesheet. You will also need an edged pen.

1 A square-edged pen will give you thick verticals…

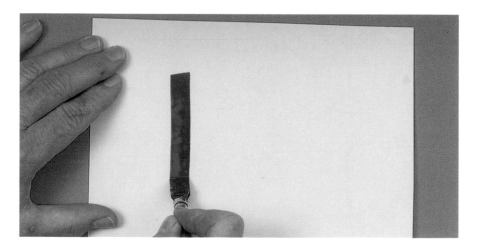

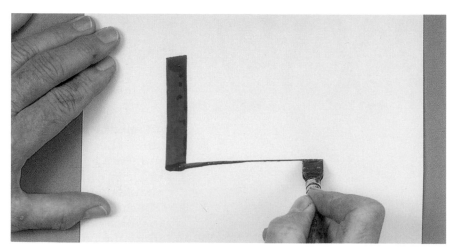

2 …and thin horizontals. These strokes give Uncial and Half-Uncial Letters their special character.

3 An alternative is to use an oblique-edged pen whose slant slopes in the opposite way to the slanted pen used to write Rustic Letters. Hold it as you would a square-edged pen. This too will produce thick verticals and thin horizontals.

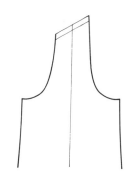

Slanted pen for Rustic Letters

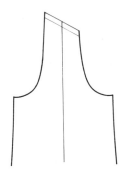

Slanted pen for Uncial and Half-Uncial Letters

4 Always attempt to keep the letter shapes rounded.

5 Copy the alphabet of Uncial Letters shown here. The numbers tell you the order in which you should do the strokes. The arrows show you in which direction to move the pen.

ABCDEFGHIJ
KLMNOPQR
STUVWXYZ

abcde abcde abcde abcde abcde

6 In order to learn the letter shapes more quickly and to build up your confidence, start by tracing them. After a few attempts, try writing them freehand.

7 Copy this alphabet of Half-Uncial Letters. Take any ascending strokes up above the body of the letters 'b', 'd', 'f', 'h', 'k', and 'l'. Allow the tails or descending strokes of the letters 'g', 'j', 'p', 'q' and 'y' to go below the body of these letters.

abcdefghij

klmmnopq

rstuvwxyz

In the ninth century AD, a Round Hand script developed. It was called the *Carolingian Minuscule*. This form of pen lettering was quicker to write than some of the earlier writing hands. It was produced with a square-edged pen (usually a quill but sometimes a reed) which was held with its writing edge at an angle of approximately 30° to the horizontal writing line.

This style of writing was used by the scribes who wrote manuscript books throughout the ninth, tenth and eleventh centuries AD (800-1000). It began to change its character, however, until it led to the Gothic style. Many present-day calligraphers write a modern version of this Round Hand.

How to write Round Hand script
Sit comfortably at your table with your writing board sloping at the correct angle. Once again the paper on which you intend to write should be placed on top of your guidesheet.

1 Take a square-edged pen, as before.

2 Practise writing the letters, remembering to hold the pen at a constant angle of 30° to the writing line. Never let this angle change. Try to write slowly and smoothly. Develop a relaxed rhythm.

ABCDEFGHIJK
LMNOPQRSTUV
WXYZ.

3 Make the letters round in shape. Try copying this alphabet of capitals.

4 Before you try writing this lower-case alphabet, you may like to practise each individual letter by following the examples shown on page 21.

abcdefghij
klmnopqr
stuvwxyz.

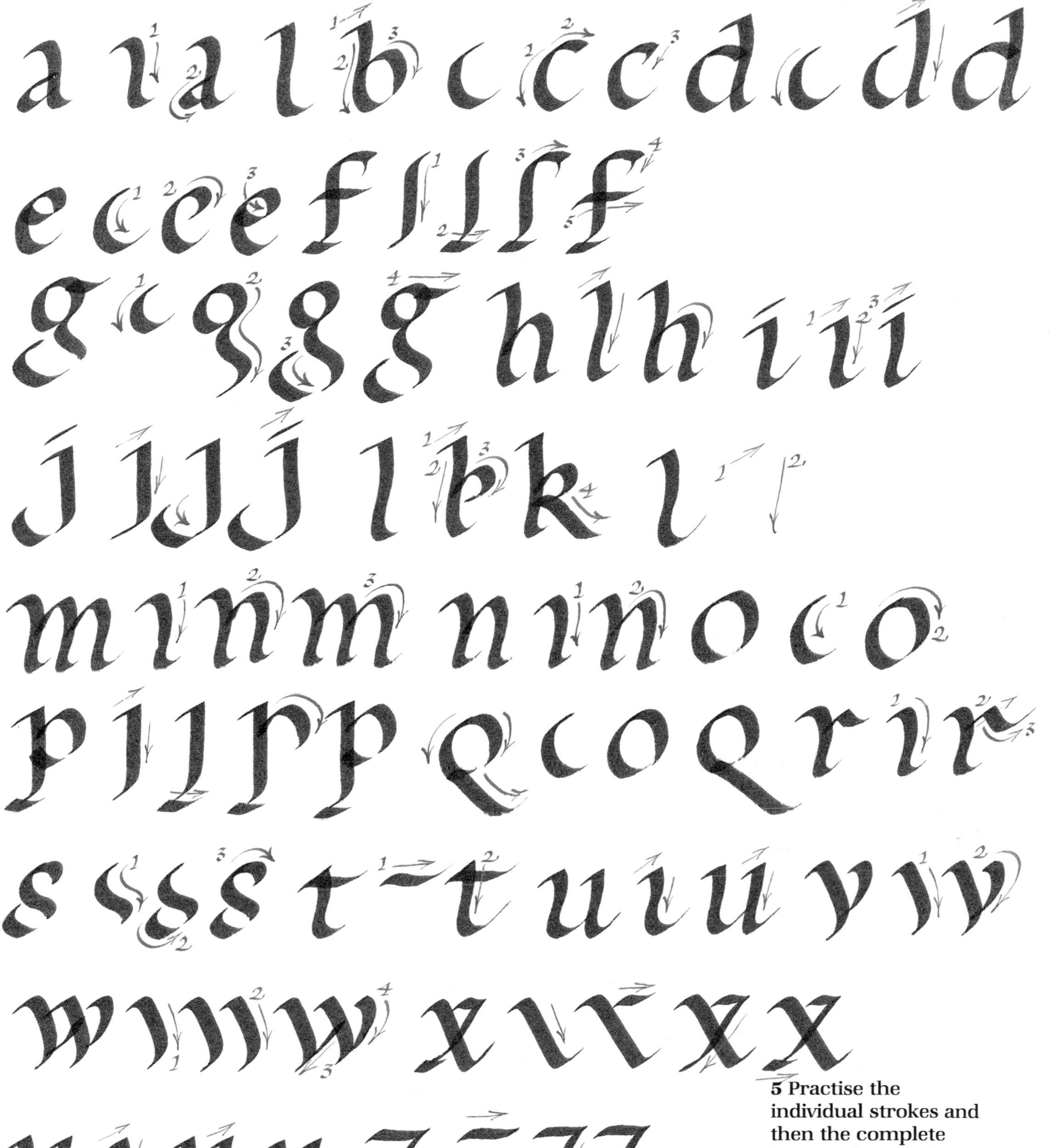

a a a l b b c c c d d d

e e c e f l l f

g g g g h h i i i

j j j j l k k l l

m m m n n n o c o

p l l p p q c q r i r

s s s s t t u i i y y

w w w w x i x x

y i y y z z z

5 Practise the individual strokes and then the complete letters. The numbers tell you the order in which you should do the strokes. The arrows show you in which direction to move the pen.

6 A pattern of freely written Round Hand Letters.

In the eleventh and twelfth centuries the Round Hands of the ninth and tenth centuries gradually changed. They began to lose their roundness, becoming much stiffer and straighter in shape. By the thirteenth century the new, so-called 'Gothic' letters had only a few curves. Gothic lettering done in the fifteenth century consists of straight lines which tend to be squashed closer and closer together. Some words appear to be a series of upright straight strokes. They are often very difficult to read.

How to write Gothic Black Letters

Sit comfortably at your table with your writing board sloping at the correct angle. The paper on which you intend to write should be placed on top of your guidesheet.

1 Take a square-edged pen and hold it with its writing edge at an angle of 30° to the writing line.

2 Here a poster pen is being used. Notice how effective and varied the ink makes the letters.

3 Look at this lower-case alphabet of Early Gothic Black Letters. Notice that they are made with straight pen lines. Try to copy this style. If you wish to make it easier, place a sheet of paper over the example and trace it.

4 This alphabet shows Late Gothic Black Letters. Examples of how some of the letters are formed are shown below.

Parchment is a natural animal skin which has been prepared so that a calligrapher can write and paint on it. In the medieval monasteries the monks used calfskin, sheepskin and goatskin. These materials are now expensive to buy. You may, however, be able to obtain a few small sample pieces to use at school or at home.

When you write to a parchment manufacturer (see page 38 for further details) explain (a) that you are learning to do calligraphy and decorated letters and wish to try working on parchment, and (b) that you are anxious to buy one or two small samples on which to experiment (10cm x 15cm, 4″ x 6″ would be fine).

Preparing parchment
When you receive parchment samples you will need to prepare them. Natural skin is resistant to water and therefore difficult to write on. Try writing with a square-ended pen and ink in one corner of a piece of parchment. If you use a calligraphy ink you may find it will work. Usually, however, you will need to 'pounce' the material with a little pumice powder (see pictures **2** and **3**).

1 Cutting small pieces of parchment from a goatskin.

2 Take a pinch of pumice powder and sprinkle it on to the parchment.

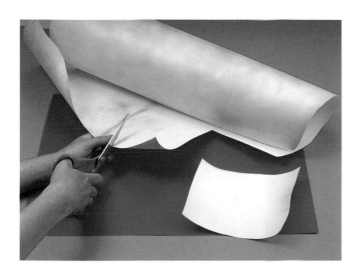

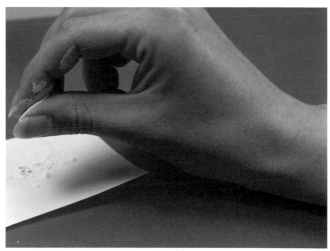

abcde abcde abcde abcde abcde

3 Using small, circular movements, rub the pumice powder gently but firmly over the surface of the parchment with your fingertips. (If you need to pounce a large piece of parchment, rub the pumice powder on to it with the ball of your thumb).

4 Gently sweep any pumice residue off the parchment. Then take a pinch of powdered resin (called Sandarach) and repeat processes **2, 3** and **4.**

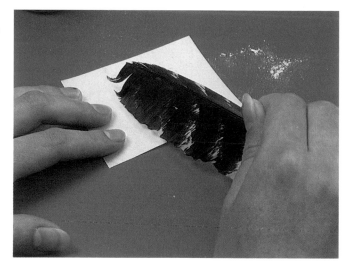

5 A professional calligrapher sometimes uses a small bag made from a piece of wash leather. This is dipped into the resin so that it picks up a small amount and then…

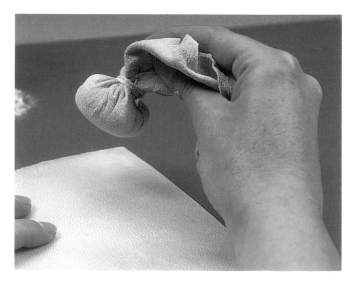

6 ...it is dabbed on to the writing surface of the parchment or vellum.

Writing on parchment

Once the writing surface of the parchment is prepared, you will need to rule in some faint guidelines. Follow the example on the guidesheet on page 10.

Remember that the size of the edged pen you use will affect the size of the letters you write. Try a No 2 or a No 3 Round Hand metal nib, or a quill pen if you have cut one.

Dip your metal nib or quill into the ink, then remove it slowly. This will ensure that you do not pick up too much ink which could cause the pen to flood on the surface of the parchment.

7 It is best to use a sloping board. Write slowly and carefully. Make some pen patterns then write an alphabet. Go on to write Gothic Letters, Uncials, Half-Uncials and Round Hand.

Designing a decorated letter

The pages of medieval manuscript books were often brilliantly decorated with gold leaf and bright colours. This decoration usually took the form of decorated letters and borders.

Here is one way of producing a decorated letter. Work on a small piece of good-quality white paper or parchment. You will also need a pencil, a ruler and fibre-tipped pens or paints.

1 In this eighth-century Celtic manuscript you can see how well a decorated letter relates to lines of Half-Uncial writing.

2 In the twelfth century, illuminated manuscripts often incorporated decorated letters on pages of Gothic lettering. Burnished gold and bright paints made them look rich and colourful.

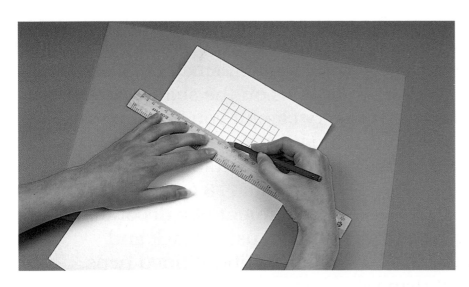

3 Using the pencil, draw a square 8cm x 8cm. Mark 1cm lengths on all four sides of the square using small dots. Join up the dots to give you a grid of sixty-four small squares.

4 Choose one capital letter and draw it carefully but boldly in pencil on to your squared grid.

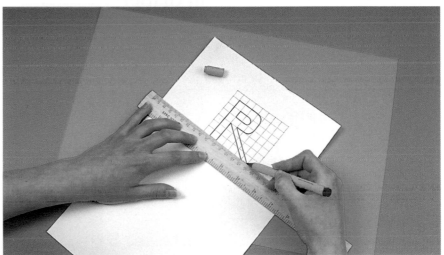

5 Select a colour for the letter and two contrasting colours for the small squares so that the letter sits against a two-colour background pattern.

The pattern shown in pictures **3**, **4** and **5** is called a *diaper pattern*. Medieval scribes often used this when decorating their manuscript books and they would 'burnish' some of the gold work, when it was used, in order to make it shine brightly.

You can make a decorated letter look very attractive by adding touches of white or colour to it or to the small diaper squares. First mix small amounts of thick paint then, using a small brush, paint small dots, squares or lines on the shapes. If you are very careful you could even give the large square in which the letter sits a coloured outline. Pictures **6**, **7**, **8** and **9** show the development of a decorated letter 'h' using black and coloured fibre-tipped pens.

6

7

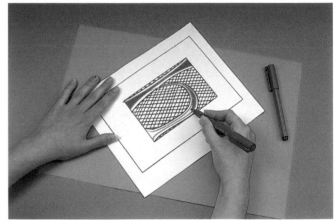

8

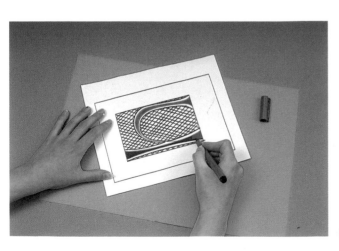

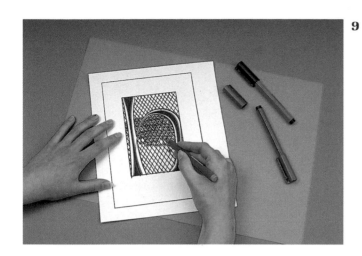

9

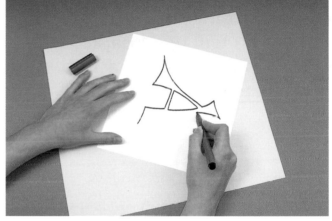

10 (Below) Draw a large capital letter such as this 'A' with a black fibre-tipped pen.

11 (Above) Add some decoration to the letter.

13 (Left) Here are some decorated letters being completed by a student. They are copied from an Irish Celtic manuscript of the eighth century AD.

12 (Above) Complete the letter by colouring it in appropriate colours.

In a great number of illuminated manuscripts the written areas of text were surrounded with decorated borders. These borders were usually rich in colour and pattern.

Design and colour some borders yourself. Here are two ideas. You will need paper, a ruler, a pencil and fibre-tipped pens (black and coloured).

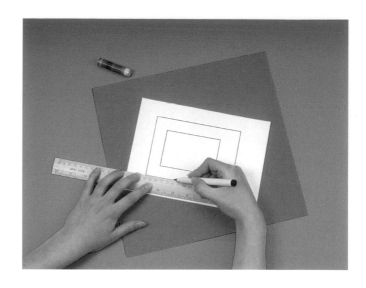

1 On the paper, draw a rectangle 15cm x 21cm (approximately 6″ x 8″). Draw another rectangle inside the first one.

2 Now draw curving lines within the shape of the border. These should look like the stems of a plant.

3 Add flowers and ivy leaves then fill in the spaces with smaller stems and dots. Colour in the whole pattern. Add some lines of pen lettering or a large decorated letter in the inside space.

4 The completed drawing.

This border is derived from fourteenth- and fifteenth-century French manuscripts. In these the scribes drew the curving stems, flowers and leaves with very fine lines, adding to them colour and burnished spots of gold.

5 This time, instead of drawing flowers and stems in the border, draw a series of small squares.

6 Invent a pattern in the squares using straight lines, as shown, or curved lines and circles. Colour your pattern.

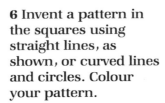

You have learned how to write different styles of pen lettering, how to use parchment and how to design simple decorated letters and borders. Now develop your own versions of some of the ideas, or try new ones. Here are some suggestions to help you.

1 Draw a large capital letter.

2 Place a sheet of tracing paper over the letter and trace its outline.

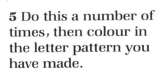

3 Take your tracing and place it over the original drawing so that the letter beneath appears in a different position. Trace the letter again, this time in its new position.

4 Move your tracing again until the letter beneath appears in yet another position. Trace the letter in its new position, perhaps using a different coloured pen.

5 Do this a number of times, then colour in the letter pattern you have made.

6 Draw a large bold letter and decorate one part of it with a dragon's head. This could look like a decorated animal letter from an Irish manuscript book such as the *Book of Kells*.

7 Design and colour a rectangle of letters. You could use a word or even numerals.

8 Develop other ideas based on squares and rectangles.

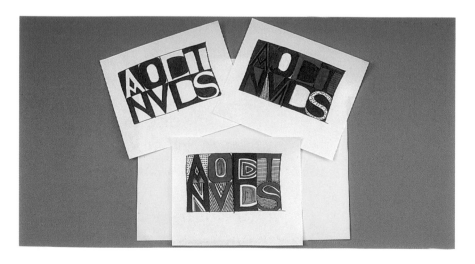

Develop what you have learned further by:

1 Producing a book of different scripts.

2 Designing a picture of decorated letters.

3 Making a poster with decorated borders.

Pictures **9** and **10** may give you some ideas.

9

10

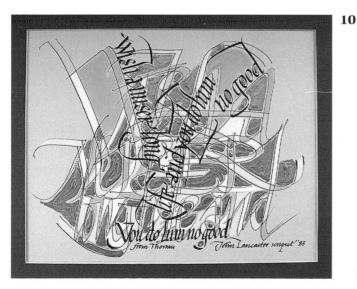

I hope that this book will have given you an interest in the art of medieval calligraphy and illumination. Try to visit a museum or library where you can see examples of early work.

Most of the materials mentioned in this book are easy to obtain. White typing paper can be bought at any stationer's shop – A4 sheets are ideal for the kind of work you will be doing. Pens, inks, rulers, pencils etc can usually be found in local stores.

The following suppliers are very helpful:

L. Cornelissen & Son Ltd
105 Great Russell Street,
London WC1 3RY
Tel: 020 7636 1045
Fax: 020 7636 3655
e-mail: info@cornelissen.com
website: www.cornelissen.com

Blots Pen & Ink Supplies
14 Lyndhurst Avenue,
Prestwich, Manchester M25 0GF
Tel & Fax: 0161 740 6916
E-mail: sales@blotspens.co.uk
Online catalogue:
www.blotspens.co.uk

Art Express
Design House,
Sizers Court
Yeadon LS19 6DP
Tel: 0113 234 0800
Freephone: 0800 7314185
www.artexpress.co.uk

Falkiner Fine Papers
76 Southampton Row
London WC1B 4AR
Tel: 020 7831 1151
Fax: 020 7430 1248
e-mail: falkiner@ic24.net

Where to see medieval manuscripts
Here is a list of some places where you can see manuscript books:

The Bodleian Library, Oxford
www.bodley.ox.ac.uk

The British Library, London
www.bl.uk

The Courtauld Institute, London
www.courtauld.ac.uk

Durham Cathedral, Durham
www.durhamcathedral.co.uk

The Fitzwilliam Museum, Cambridge
www.fitzmuseum.cam.ac.uk

Hereford Cathedral, Hereford
www.herefordcathedral.co.uk

Trinity College, Dublin
www.tcd.ie/Library

The Victoria and Albert Museum, London
www.vam.ac.uk

York Minister, York
www.yorkminster.org

A study of the history of lettering and calligraphy is fascinating. It is, however, a vast area, and in order to make it as simple as possible for you it is presented here as a series of notes.

Three broad stages of development

PICTOGRAMS

Pictograms are simplified pictures used as a form of writing. Twenty thousand years ago, prehistoric people drew these pictures on cave walls.

Hieroglyphics

An hieroglyph is a picture of an object which is used to represent a word, sound or syllable. These formalised pictures were used 5,000 years ago by the Egyptians.

IDEOGRAMS

Ideograms are stylised pictures which convey ideas.

This ideogram of an eye crying means 'grief' or 'sorrow'.

This ideogram of a shining sun means 'daytime', 'brightness' or 'heat'.

PHONOGRAMS

Phonograms are written characters which represent sounds. They were first developed by the Sumerians around 3,000 BC.

Sumerian   c. 3,000 BC
Wedge-shaped images

Greek and Etruscan   c. 800 BC
The beginnings of letters as we know them

AEVSNORM

Roman   700 BC
Strong, beautiful capital letters

Medieval   400-1100 AD
Uncials

Half-Uncials

Carolingian Minuscule

Winchester

Gothic

Modern-day
1800 Italic

Modern
1900 Modern calligraphy

Ascending strokes 16, 18

Brush 4, 26, 30

Calligrapher 2, 11, 19, 25, 26, 38
Calligraphy 5, 25, 37, 38, 39
Capital letters 9, 12, 14, 20, 29, 31, 34, 39
Card 4, 7, 8
Carolingian Minuscule 19, 39
Craft knife 4

Descending strokes 16, 18
Decorated borders 6, 28, 32-33, 34, 36
Decorated letters 5, 6, 25, 28-31, 32, 34, 36
Diaper pattern 30
Dip pen 5, 12, 13

Edged pen 5, 6, 8, 9, 13, 14, 16, 17, 19, 23, 27
Elastic bands 4, 7

Fibre-tipped pens 4, 9, 12, 13, 28, 30, 31, 32

Gold (leaf) 6, 28, 30, 33
Gothic Black Letters 12, 19, 23-24, 27, 28, 39
Guidesheet 9, 10, 12, 14, 16, 19, 23, 27

Half-Uncial letters 12, 16-18, 27, 28, 39
Hieroglyphics 39

Ideograms 39
Illuminated letters/ manuscripts 6, 28, 32
Ink(s) 4, 5, 9, 23, 25, 27, 38

Lower-case letters 9, 16, 20, 24

Manuscript books 5, 6, 14, 19, 28, 30, 31, 33, 36, 38
Masking tape 4
Monks 16, 25

Paints 28, 30
Paper 4, 5, 6, 7, 8, 9, 10, 11, 12, 14, 16, 19, 23, 24, 28, 32, 38
Paper clips 4, 9
Parchment 4, 5, 6, 7, 9, 25, 26, 27, 28, 34, 38
Pen lettering 14, 19, 32, 31
Pen patterns 11, 27
Pencil 4, 28, 29, 32, 38
Pen(s) 4, 5, 6, 7, 8, 9, 11, 12, 13, 14, 15, 16, 17, 19, 21, 24, 25, 27, 35, 38
Phonograms 39
Pictograms 39
Pounce 4, 25, 26
Pouncing parchment 25-27
Pumice powder 25, 26

Quill pen 4, 5, 7, 12, 19, 27, 38

Resin 26
Roman Square Capitals 12, 12-13, 14, 15, 16, 39
Round Hand 5, 12, 19-22, 23, 27
Ruler 4, 9, 28, 32, 38
Rustic Letters 5, 8, 12, 14-15, 16, 17

Scissors 4
Scribes 2, 5, 6, 7, 9, 12, 14, 19, 30, 33
Scriptoria 2, 7
Script(s) 6, 8, 12, 16, 19, 36

Tracing paper 4, 34

Uncial Letters 5, 8, 12, 16-18, 27, 39

Vellum 4, 5, 6, 9, 27

Winchester 39
Work table 4, 7, 19, 23
Writing angle 7, 8, 13, 19, 23
Writing board 4, 7, 12, 14, 16, 19, 23, 27, 38
Writing position 7-8
Writing rhythm 11, 19

ABCDE
KLMN
STUV

f F G b l J

o p q R

y x y z

aBcde
KLMN
STUV